Christian Cross-Stitch

Abingdon Press, Nashville

ACKNOWLEDGMENTS

Designers: F. S. Davis and May Abers
Authors: May Abers, F. S. Davis, and Peggy Augustine
Photography: Sid Dorris
Framing by Nancy Johnstone

Stitchers and Finishers:

May Abers	Florence Davis
Susan Barrett	Kathy Harding
Renee Benedict	Cynthia Kennedy
Kelley Bowers	Susan Brown
Laura Bryant	Renee Ragsdale
Julie Cantrell	Hazel Reynolds
Cindy Solomon	Bernadine Shaw

Floss color numbers are by DMC Co.

CHRISTIAN CROSS-STITCH

Seventh Printing 1992

ISBN 0-687-07033-3

MANUFACTURED IN THE UNITED STATES OF AMERICA

About This Book

This book is for the many Christian women, men, and young people who wish to use cross-stitched designs to praise the Lord and the beauty of his creations. The designs have many uses: bazaar items, Christmas decorations, seasonal decorations, Sunday school gifts, prizes, and more.

Many of the designs include a suggested scripture text. Also included are an alphabet and initial letters. In addition to a wide variety of Christian symbols, some denominational emblems are included.

GENERAL INSTRUCTIONS FOR CROSS-STITCH

THE BASIC CROSS-STITCH

To make a cross-stitch, bring the needle up through a hole in the evenweave fabric at one corner of the square. Cross the square diagonally and insert the needle in hole opposite the beginning of stitch. Repeat across the row. After the half-stitch is done across the entire row, complete the stitch by crossing in the opposite direction (see diagram). Do this across the row to end up where the first stitch was started.

Make sure all stitches follow the same direction.

Occasionally a half-cross-stitch will be used to round out a corner.

This will be indicated like so: 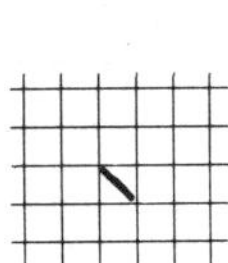

USING WASTE CANVAS

If you wish to use a cross-stitch design on a fabric which is not an evenweave cross-stitch fabric, you can accomplish this by using waste canvas.

To use waste canvas, baste the canvas to the fabric on which you wish the design to appear. Stitch the design through both pieces of material using the waste canvas as a guide. After the stitching is completed, remove basting. Using tweezers, carefully pull out the canvas threads one at a time.

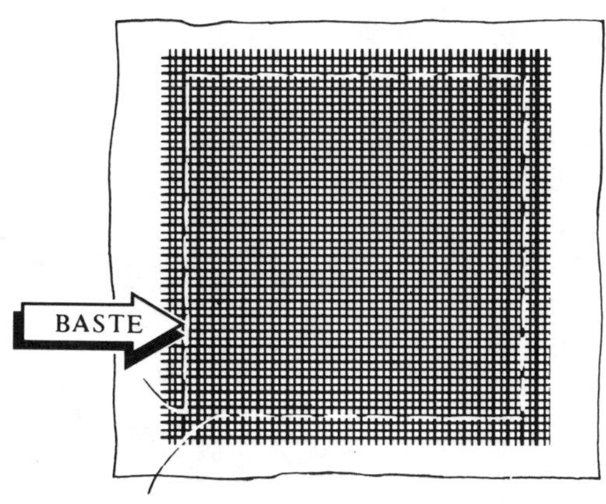

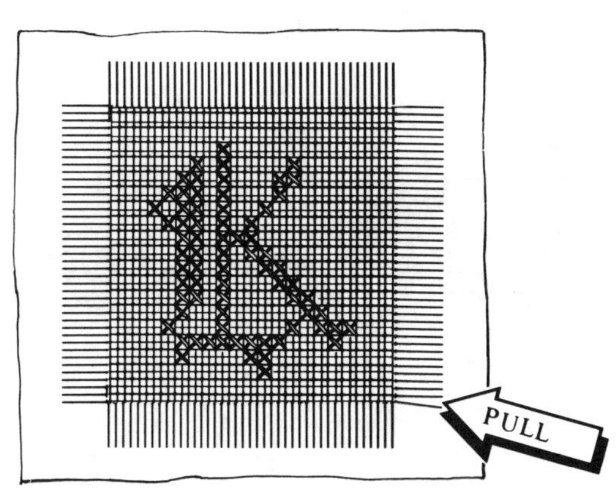

Other stitches used in this book

BACKSTITCH
A backstitch will often be specified to either outline or define a line.

STEM STITCH
Occasionally a stem stitch will be specified for outlines where an evenly curved line is needed.

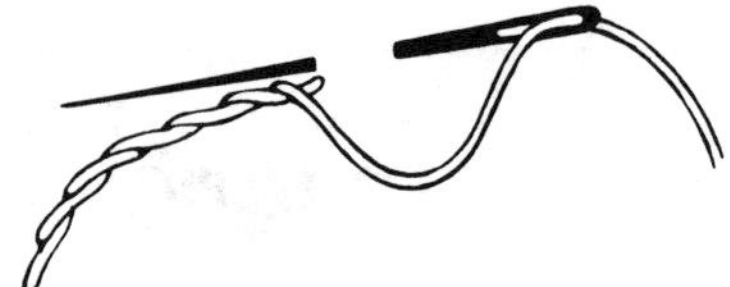

FRENCH KNOT
This stitch will be used for the center of flowers, eyes, or other such accents. To make the stitch, bring the needle up through the fabric, wrap the thread around the needle twice (see diagram). Pull the thread fairly tight around the needle. Insert the needle near the beginning of the stitch and pull through, holding thread taut while completing the stitch.

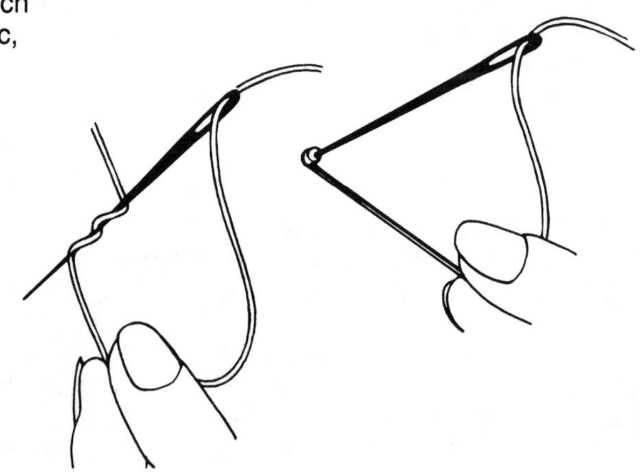

SATIN STITCH
This stitch is used to fill an area with even, straight stitches placed closely together. Be sure to keep the stitches parallel and at an even tension.

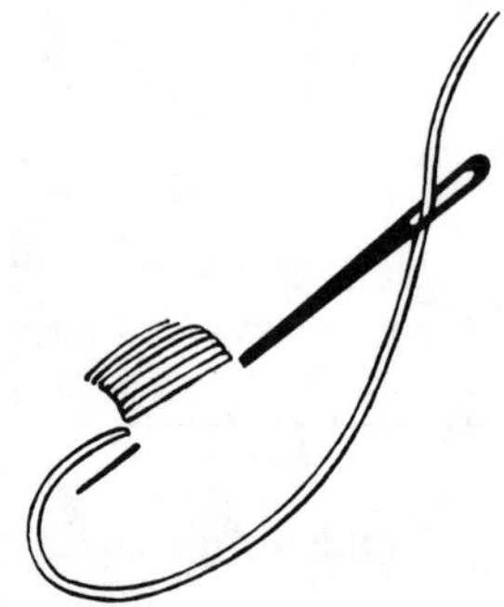

CHRISTMAS ORNAMENTS

Use the following instructions to make the Christmas ornaments shown on the cover from the designs on pages 7 and 8.

Materials you will need

Lace—about ¾-inch wide, either white or off-white
Cross-stitch fabric—18-count, either white or off-white
Backing fabric (cotton)—either solid color or with a small Christmas pattern
Quilt batting
Embroidery floss—see colors listed on pages 7 and 8
Crochet thread for hanger

Stitch the design on 18-count cross-stitch fabric, either white or off-white. Use two strands of floss for stitching. Be sure to have at least a 2-inch margin around the design when stitching.

After the design is stitched, cut out a circle 4 inches in diameter with the stitched design centered in the circle. Cut out the same size circle from fabric of either a solid color or a small Christmas print for the back of the ornament.

Cut a circle 3½ inches in diameter from quilt batting for inside the ornament. Cut 18 inches of lace for trim. The color of the lace should match the color of your cross-stitch cloth.

Fold the edges of the front and back circles under ¼-inch all around. Place the batting circle between the two fabric circles. Pin the lace between the edges of the fabric circles. Slip stitch the edges of the fabric circles together, catching the lace between them.

For the hanger, chain stitch a chain about 4¾ inches long, attaching both ends to lace at center top.

FLOSS

Floss color numbers given are by DMC Co. (Conversion charts for other brands are available at most craft shops.) Number of floss strands used will depend on fabric count, as 2 strands for 22 count and 3 strands for 14 count. Use 1 less strand of floss for accent stitches than number chosen for cross-stitch.

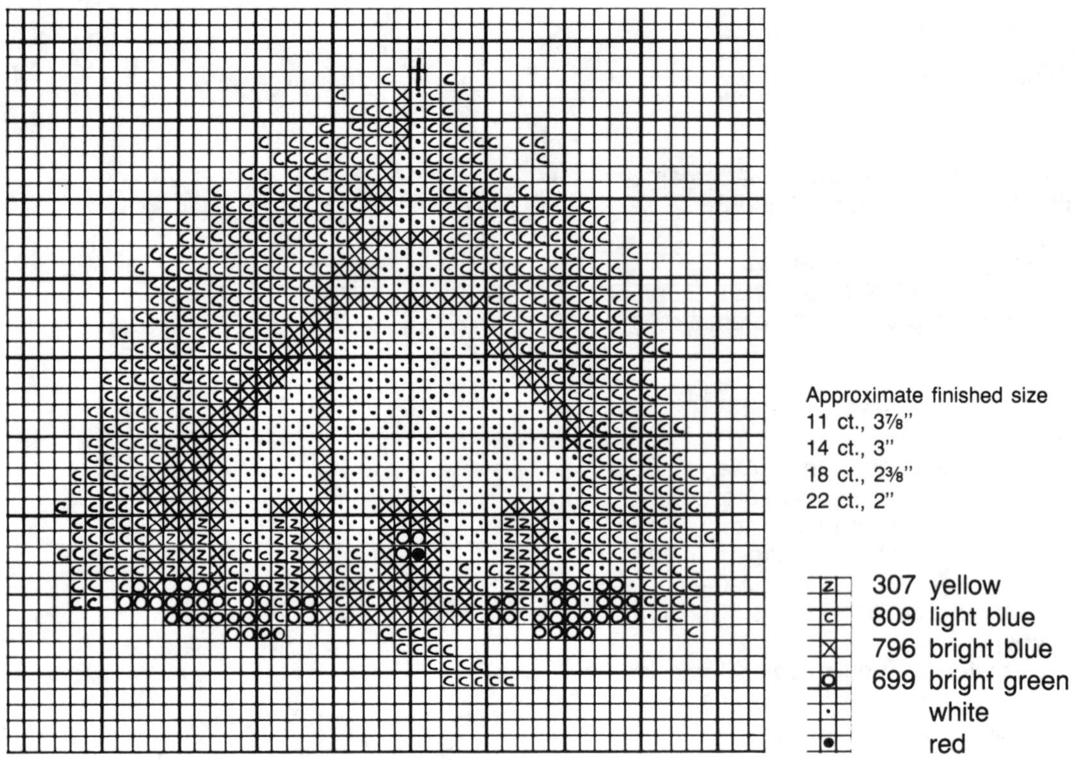

Approximate finished size
11 ct., 3⅞"
14 ct., 3"
18 ct., 2⅜"
22 ct., 2"

Symbol	Color
z	307 yellow
c	809 light blue
X	796 bright blue
O	699 bright green
·	white
●	red

See instructions for Christmas ornaments on page 5.

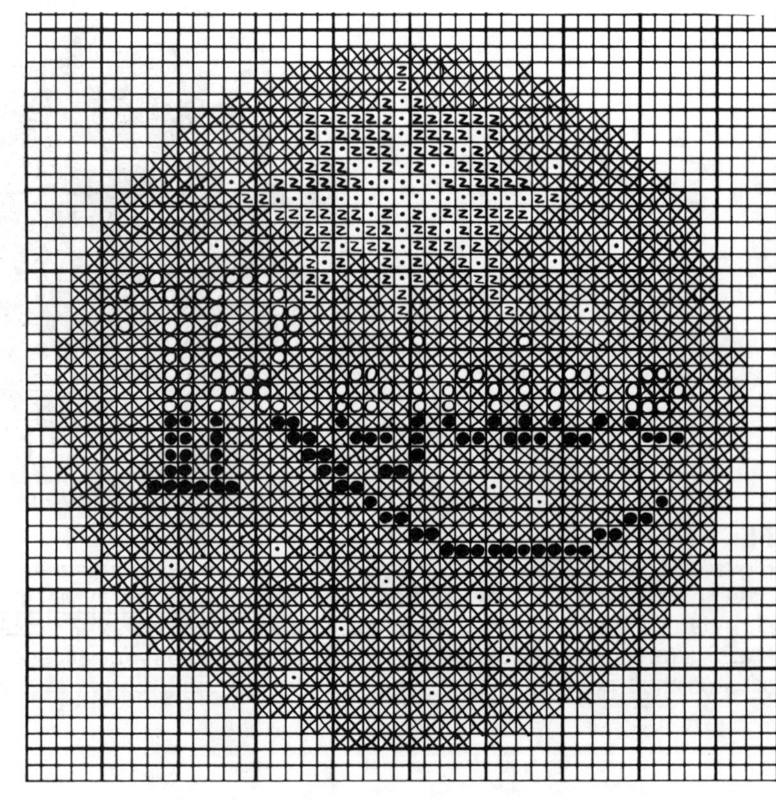

Approximate finished size
11 ct., 4⅛"
14 ct., 3¼"
18 ct., 2½"
22 ct., 2"

Symbol	Color
O	307 yellow
●	741 yellow orange
z	809 light blue
X	796 bright blue
·	white

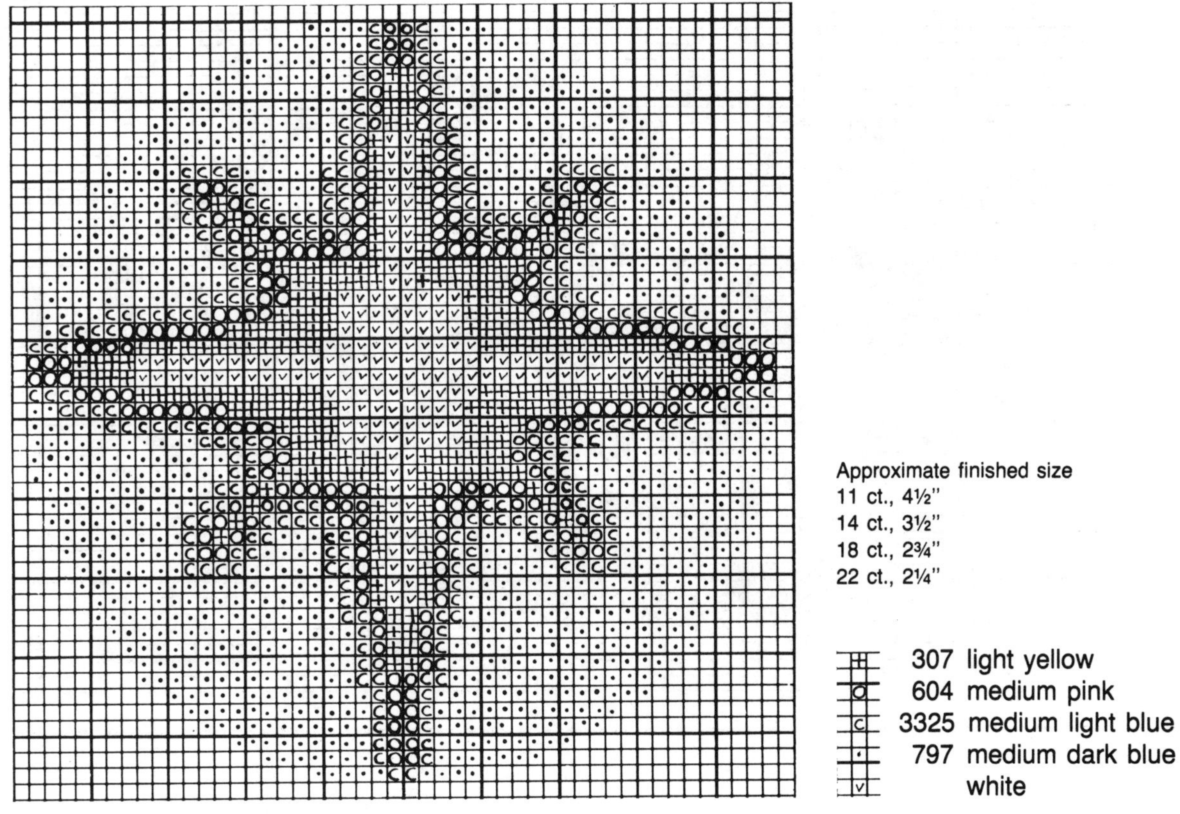

See instructions for Christmas ornaments on page 5.

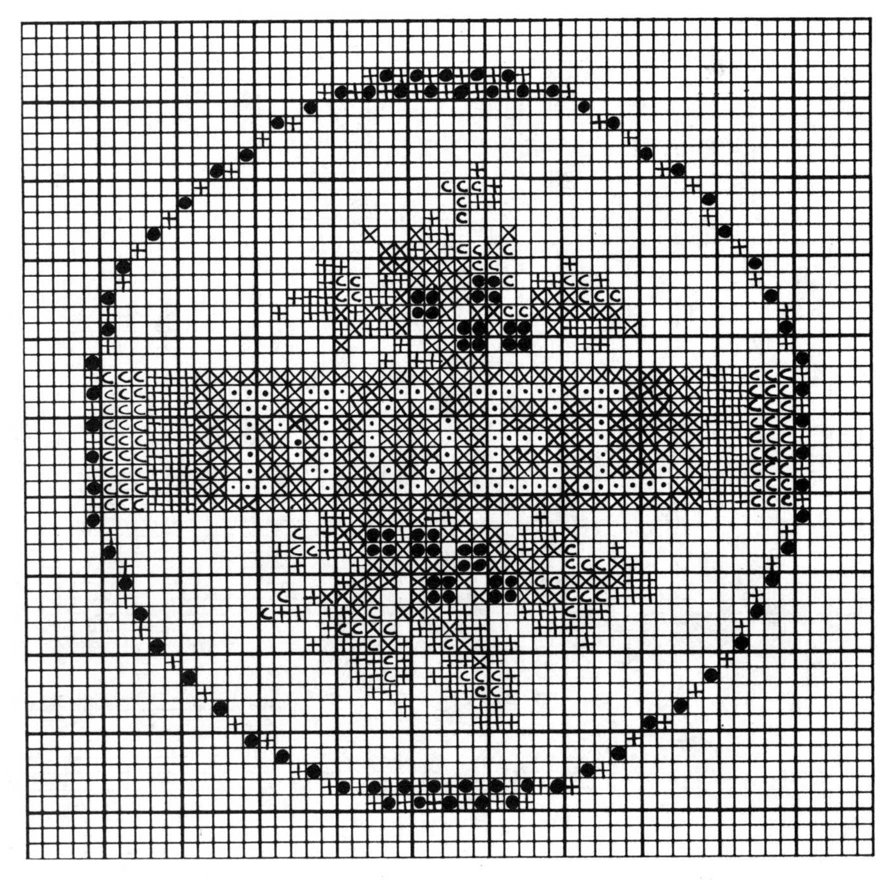

Approximate finished size
11 ct., 4½"
14 ct., 3½"
18 ct., 2¾"
22 ct., 2¼"

699 bright dark green
702 medium green
966 light green
666 bright red
white

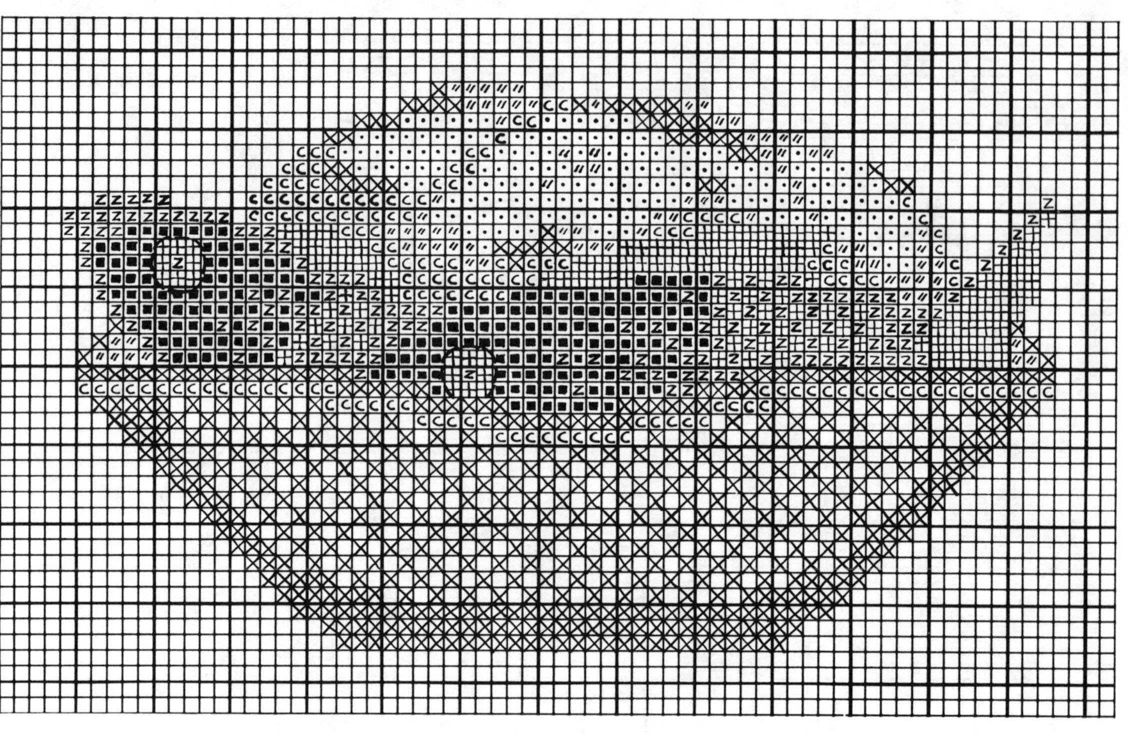

The lamb symbolizes Jesus as the Lamb of God, who in his life, death, and resurrection takes our sin on himself.

Behold the Lamb of God! John 1:36

Approximate finished size
11 ct., 6½" x 4⅛"
14 ct., 5⅛" x 3¼"
18 ct., 4" x 2½"
22 ct., 3¼" x 2"

Symbol	Color
╪	445 light yellow
·	444 bright yellow
Z	472 light yellow/green
"	906 medium green
X	904 medium dark green
▨	318 silver gray (satin and stem stitch)
O	white (French knot)

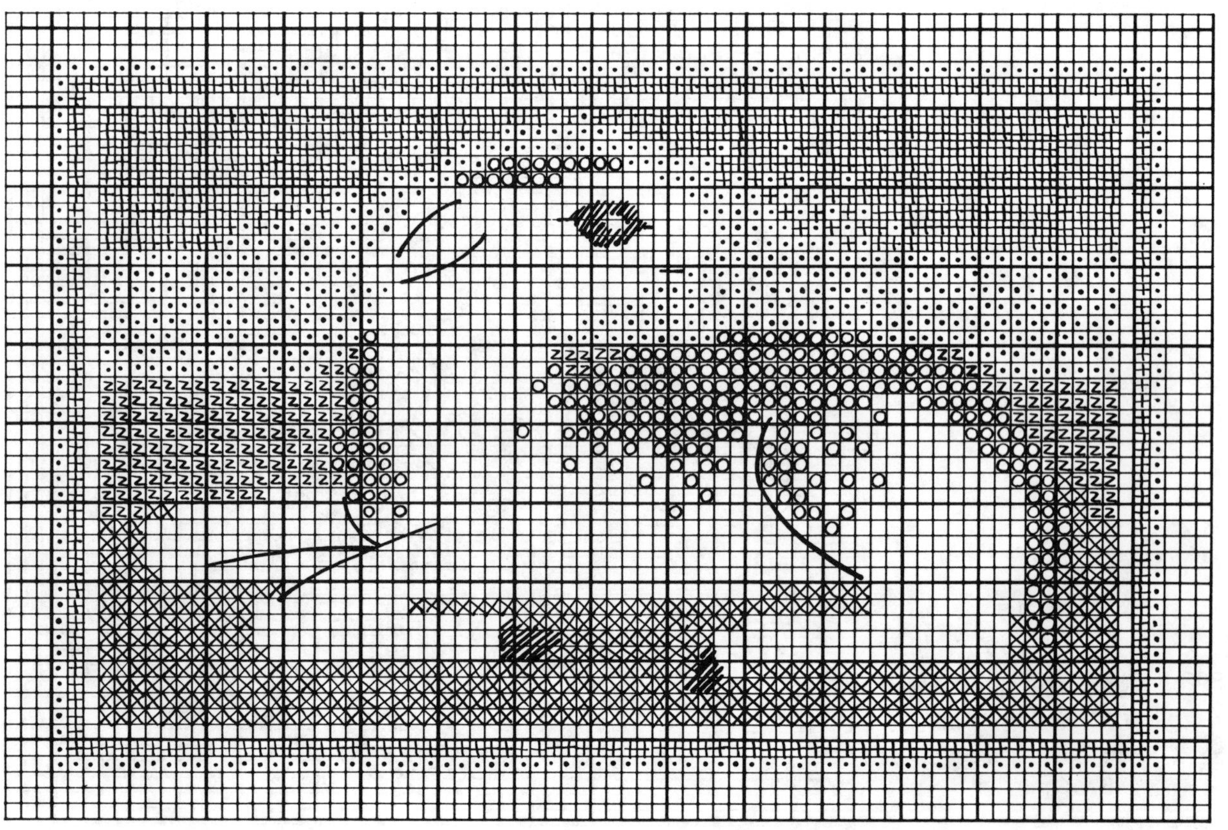

The loaves and fish represent the feeding of the five thousand.

Break thou the bread of life

Symbol	Color
·	739 light beige
X	729 gold
c	301 dark burnt orange
■	813 medium light blue
+	955 medium light green
″	722 light orange
z	824 medium dark blue (outline eyes using one strand)

Approximate finished size
11 ct., 5⅞" x 3¼"
14 ct., 4⅝" x 2½"
18 ct., 3½" x 2"
22 ct., 3" x 1⅝"

Noah's ark represents salvation, and the dove with an olive branch is the symbol of peace.

Behold, I establish my covenant with you.
Genesis 9:9

Symbol	Color
z	986 green (with backstitch stem)
X	809 medium light blue
c	797 medium blue (with backstitch wings and tail)
·	738 tan
+	433 brown
●	310 black (French knot eyes, and straight stitch beak)

Approximate finished size
11 ct., 5⅝" x 6½"
14 ct., 4½" x 5⅛"
18 ct., 3½" x 4"
22 ct., 2¾" x 3¼"

Clusters of grapes stand for the Holy Communion because the wine or grape juice used in the service is made from grapes. Since bread is made from wheat, wheat also symbolizes the Lord's Supper.

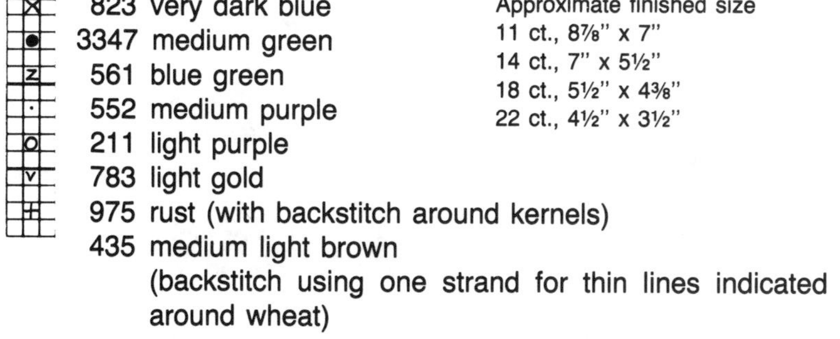

823 very dark blue
3347 medium green
561 blue green
552 medium purple
211 light purple
783 light gold
975 rust (with backstitch around kernels)
435 medium light brown (backstitch using one strand for thin lines indicated around wheat)

Approximate finished size
11 ct., 8⅞" x 7"
14 ct., 7" x 5½"
18 ct., 5½" x 4⅜"
22 ct., 4½" x 3½"

The shell spilling drops of water symbolizes baptism, the way we are marked as followers of Christ.

He that believeth and is baptized shall be saved. Mark 16:16

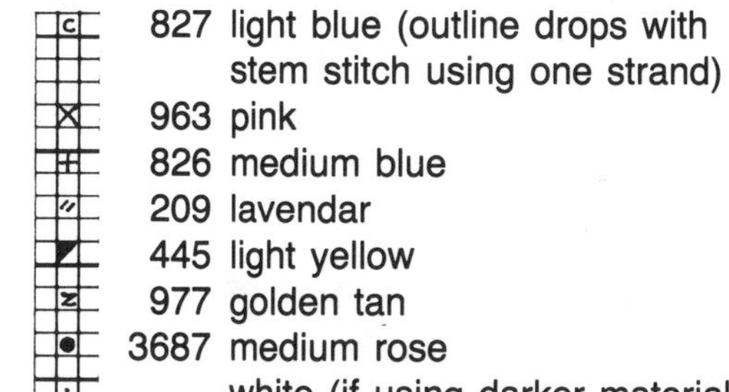

827 light blue (outline drops with stem stitch using one strand)
963 pink
826 medium blue
209 lavendar
445 light yellow
977 golden tan
3687 medium rose
white (if using darker material)

Approximate finished size
11 ct., 7⅜" x 6½"
14 ct., 5¾" x 5⅛"
18 ct., 4½" x 4"
22 ct., 3⅝" x 3¼"

Joy to the world!

Approximate finished size
11 ct., 6⅞" x 6½"
14 ct., 5⅜" x 5⅛"
18 ct., 4¼" x 4"
22 ct., 3⅜" x 3¼"

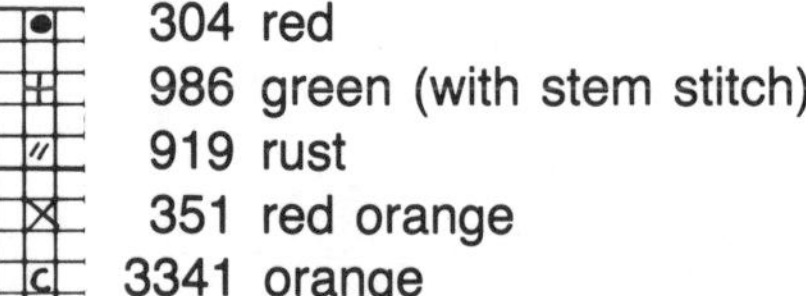

304 red
986 green (with stem stitch)
919 rust
351 red orange
3341 orange
744 yellow

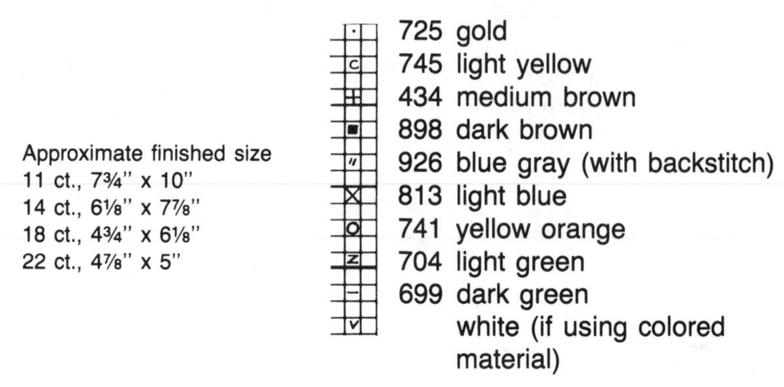

The cross surrounded by lilies represents the Resurrection. The lily bulb lies dormant in the ground, yet from it new life is released.

Approximate finished size
11 ct., 7¾" x 10"
14 ct., 6⅛" x 7⅞"
18 ct., 4¾" x 6⅛"
22 ct., 4⅞" x 5"

725 gold
745 light yellow
434 medium brown
898 dark brown
926 blue gray (with backstitch)
813 light blue
741 yellow orange
704 light green
699 dark green
white (if using colored material)

The French word for "Christmas" is Noel.

Approximate finished size
11 ct., 1¾" x 6¼"
14 ct., 1⅜" x 4⅞"
18 ct., 1" x 3¾"
22 ct., ⅞" x 3⅛"

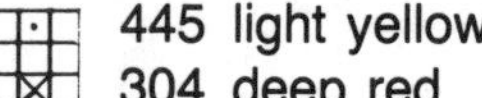

445 light yellow
304 deep red
725 gold
699 bright dark green
704 light green

Suitable for bookmark.

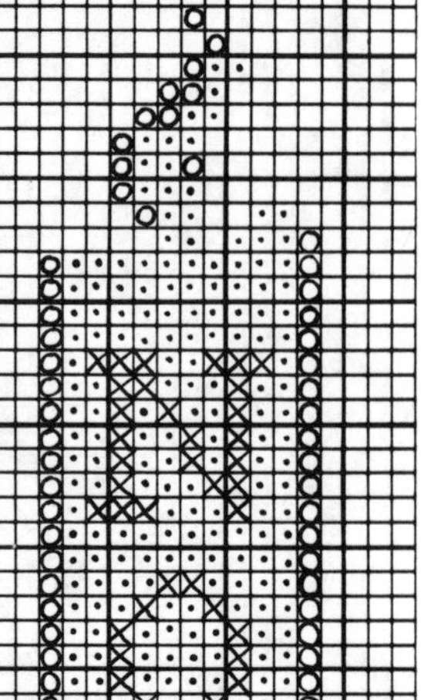

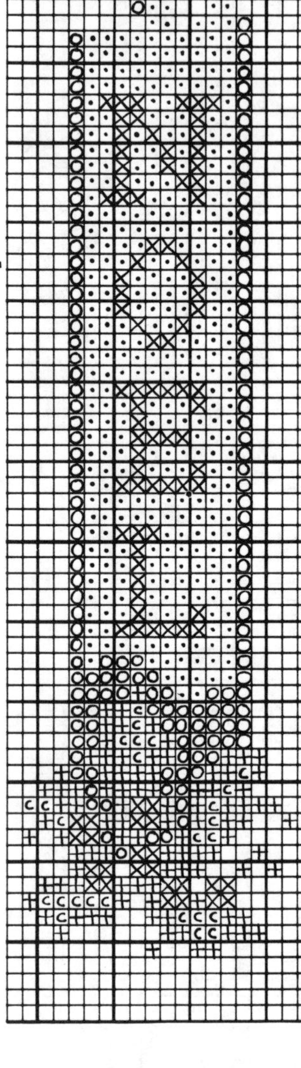

The cup is a symbol of the Lord's Supper.

This do in remembrance of me.
Luke 22:19

Approximate finished size
11 ct., 5¼" x 5⅞"
14 ct., 4⅛" x 4⅝"
18 ct., 3¼" x 3½"
22 ct., 2⅝" x 3"

445 light yellow
742 yellow orange (backstitch rays)
721 orange
347 red/rust

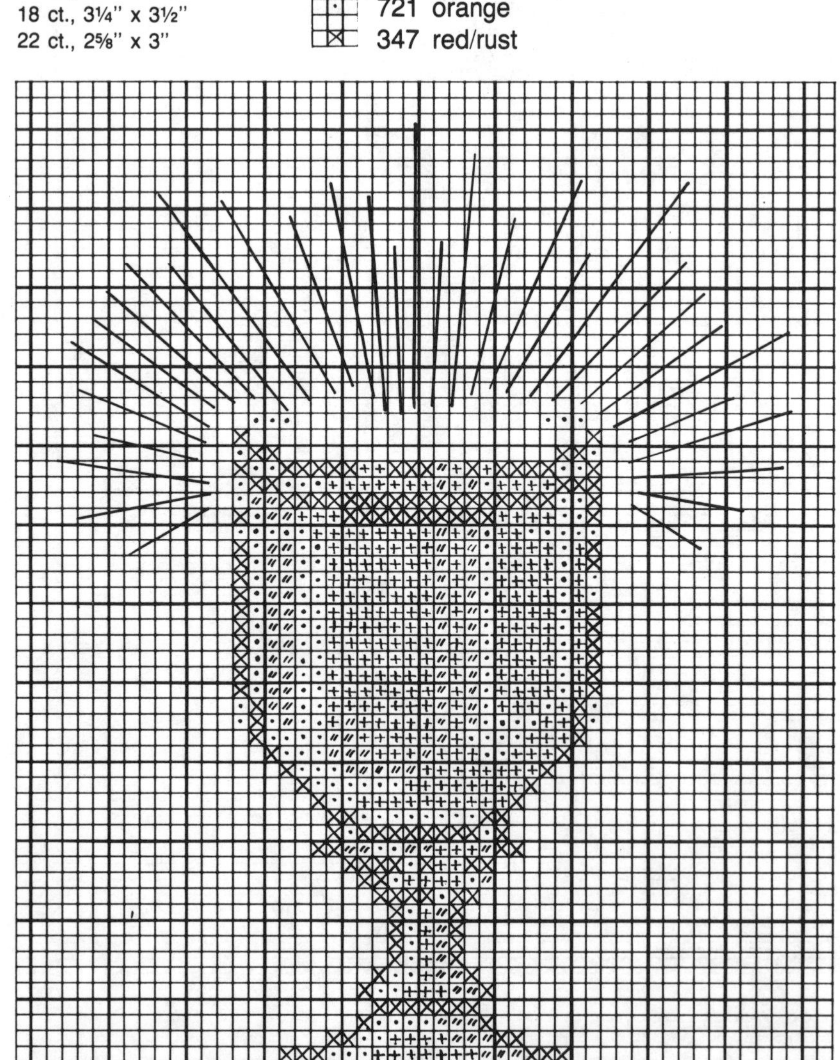

The star is used here to represent the great light that shone when the angels told the shepherds of Christ's birth.

Approximate finished size
11 ct., 6¾" x 11½"
14 ct., 5⅜" x 9"
18 ct., 4⅛" x 7"
22 ct., 3⅜" x 5¾"

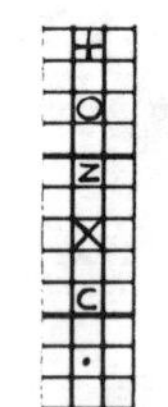

445 light yellow
3689 medium pink
208 medium purple
991 dark blue green
809 medium light blue
311 medium dark blue
310 black

Approximate finished size
11 ct., 6½" x 6¾"
14 ct., 5" x 5¼"
18 ct., 4" x 4⅛"
22 ct., 3¼" x 3⅜"

Symbol	Color
O	727 light yellow
●	727 light yellow (French knots)
X	3325 medium light blue
∩	3340 orange
·	986 medium dark green

The blossom of the dogwood tree represents the passion and death of Christ on the cross. The petals represent the cross, and the edging symbolizes the blood on his hands and feet. The stamen represents the crown of thorns.

Symbol	Color
·	725 yellow
X	729 gold
*	801 dark brown
●	3371 very dark brown
U	907 medium light green
◤	472 light green
∇	905 medium green
–	444 medium yellow
+	921 orange
//	815 deep red
/	321 bright red
O	754 pink beige
C	902 very dark red
Z	780 medium brown
◘	white

Approximate finished size
11 ct., 7⅝" x 8⅞"
14 ct., 6" x 7"
18 ct., 4⅝" x 5½"
22 ct., 3⅞" x 4½"

The cornucopia, or horn of plenty, reminds us to be thankful.

We give thee thanks, O Lord God. Revelation 11:17

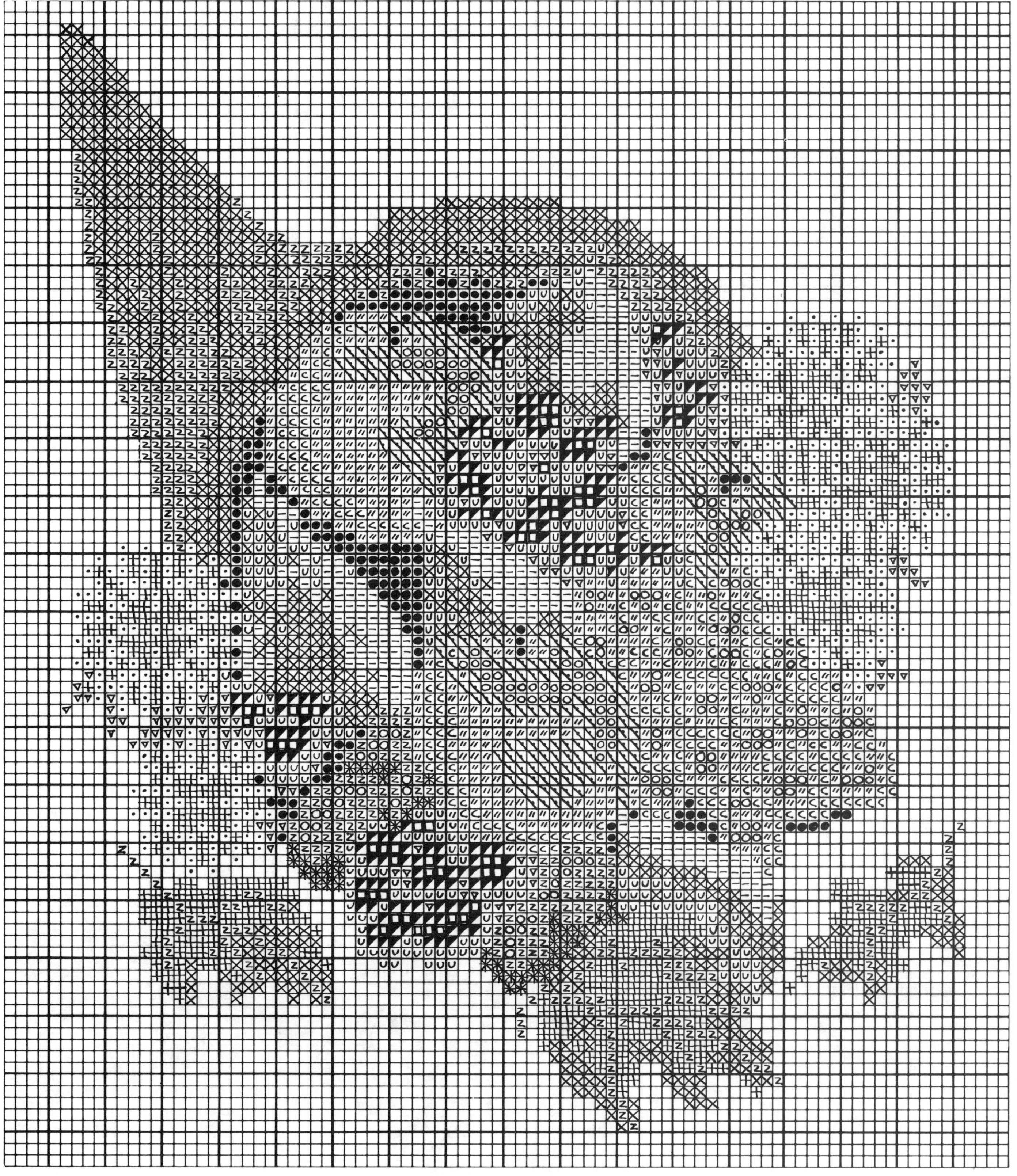

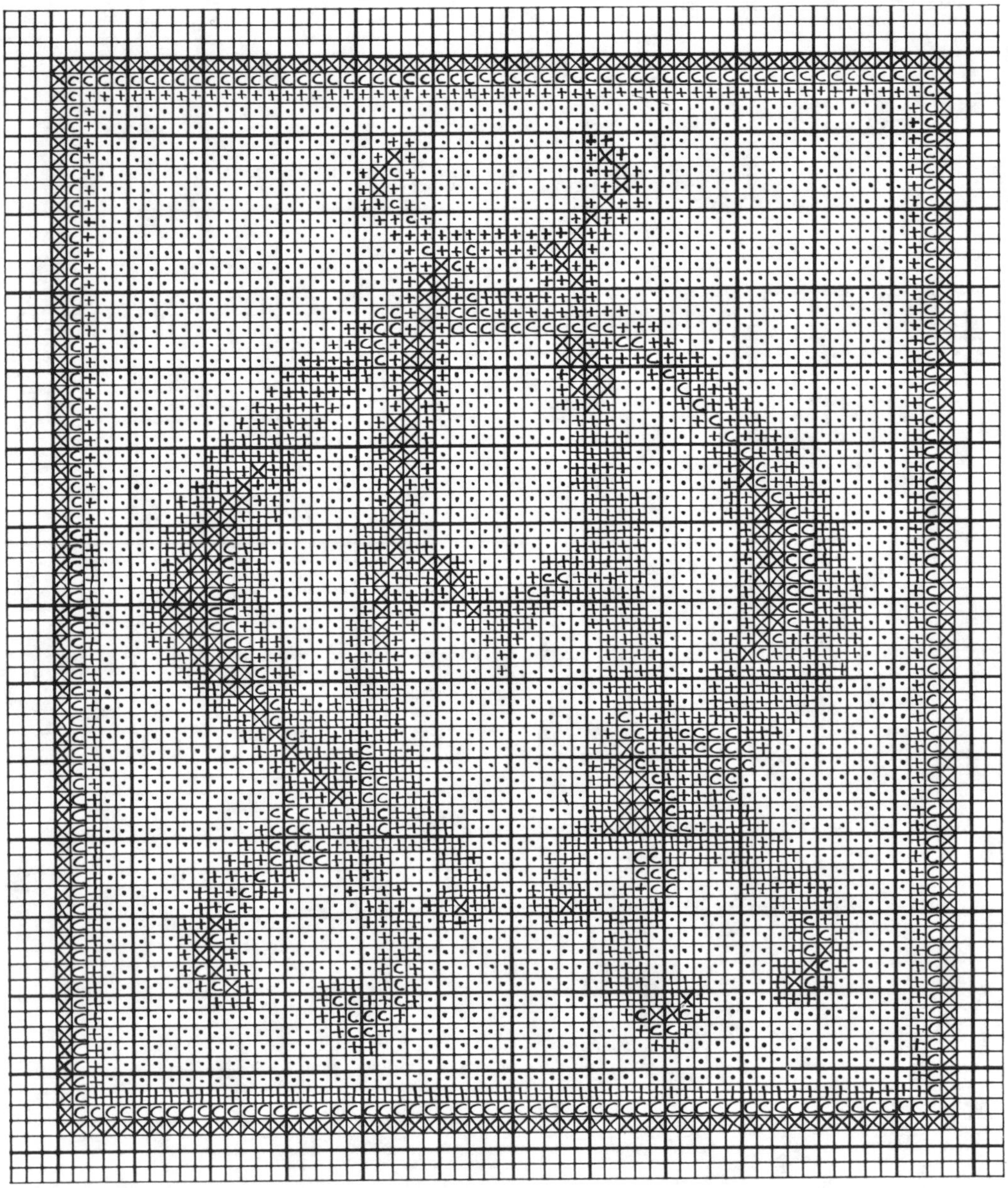

Approximate finished size
11 ct., 5⅜" x 6½"
14 ct., 4⅛" x 5"
18 ct., 3¼" x 4"
22 ct., 2⅝" x 3¼"

- 3350 red plumb
- 722 medium orange
- 742 yellow orange
- 727 yellow

Letters which look like an A and an upside down U are the first and last letters in the Greek alphabet and stand for Christ, "the beginning and the end, the first and the last" (Rev. 22:13).

Because holly is an evergreen it sometimes is used to symbolize the hope and expectance of spring. At the same time, it reminds us of the crown of thorns which Christ wore during his crucifixion. When thought of in this way, the berries represent the blood he shed for us.

Approximate finished size
(each design)
11 ct., 2"
14 ct., 1⅝"
18 ct., 1¼"
22 ct., 1"

- 666 red
- 699 dark green
- 704 light green

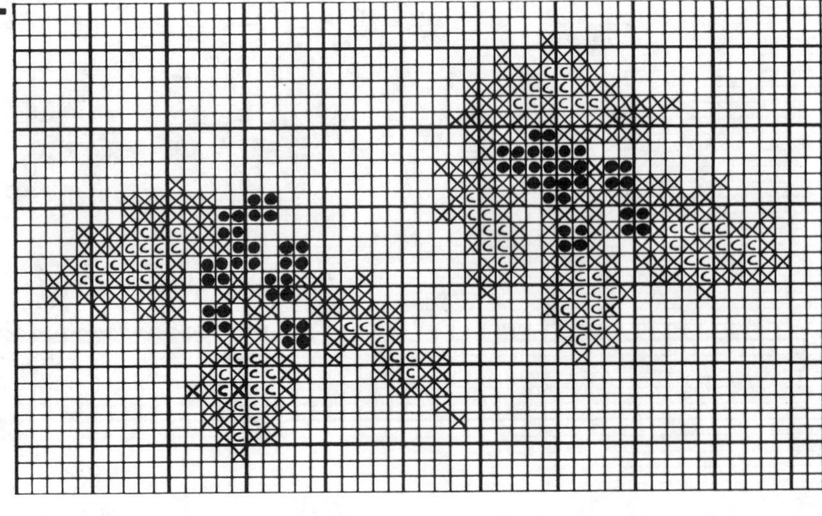

Advent means "to come." The days before Christmas are a time for Christians to prepare themselves mentally and spiritually for the coming of Christ. The round shape of the Advent wreath shows us God's never-ending love. The evergreens represent everlasting life. The large white candle represents the purity of Jesus.

O come, O come, Emmanuel

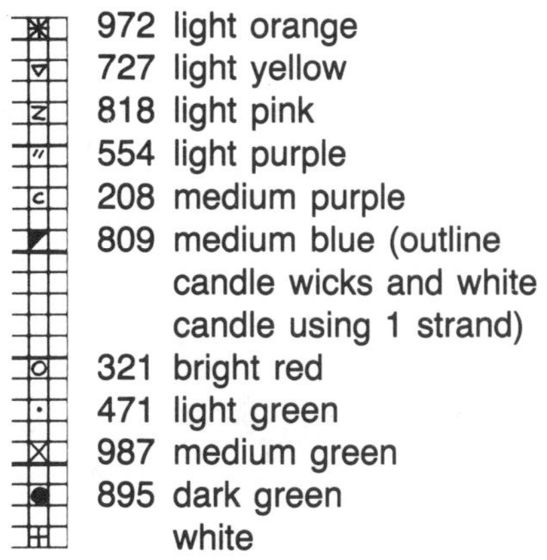

972 light orange
727 light yellow
818 light pink
554 light purple
208 medium purple
809 medium blue (outline candle wicks and white candle using 1 strand)
321 bright red
471 light green
987 medium green
895 dark green
white

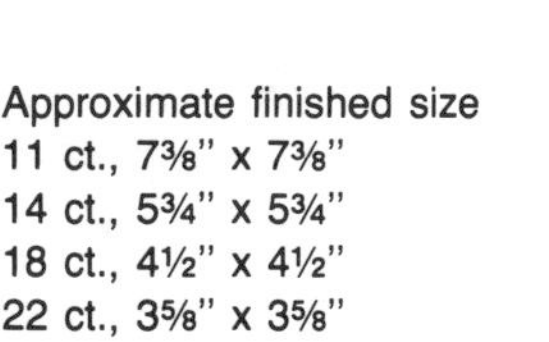

Approximate finished size
11 ct., 7⅜" x 7⅜"
14 ct., 5¾" x 5¾"
18 ct., 4½" x 4½"
22 ct., 3⅝" x 3⅝"

Approximate finished size
11 ct., 6¼" x 9½"
14 ct., 5" x 7⅝"
18 ct., 3¾" x 5¾"
22 ct., 3⅛" x 4¾"

Symbol	Color
c	820 bright blue
X	815 maroon
+	3687 dusty rose
•	800 light blue

The crown of thorns is a symbol of humiliation and suffering, plaited by the soldiers and imposed on Jesus during his trial before Pilate.

Approximate finished size
11 ct., 6½"
14 ct., 5⅛"
18 ct., 4"
22 ct., 3¼"

Symbol	Color
c	919 rust
X	53 variegated gray

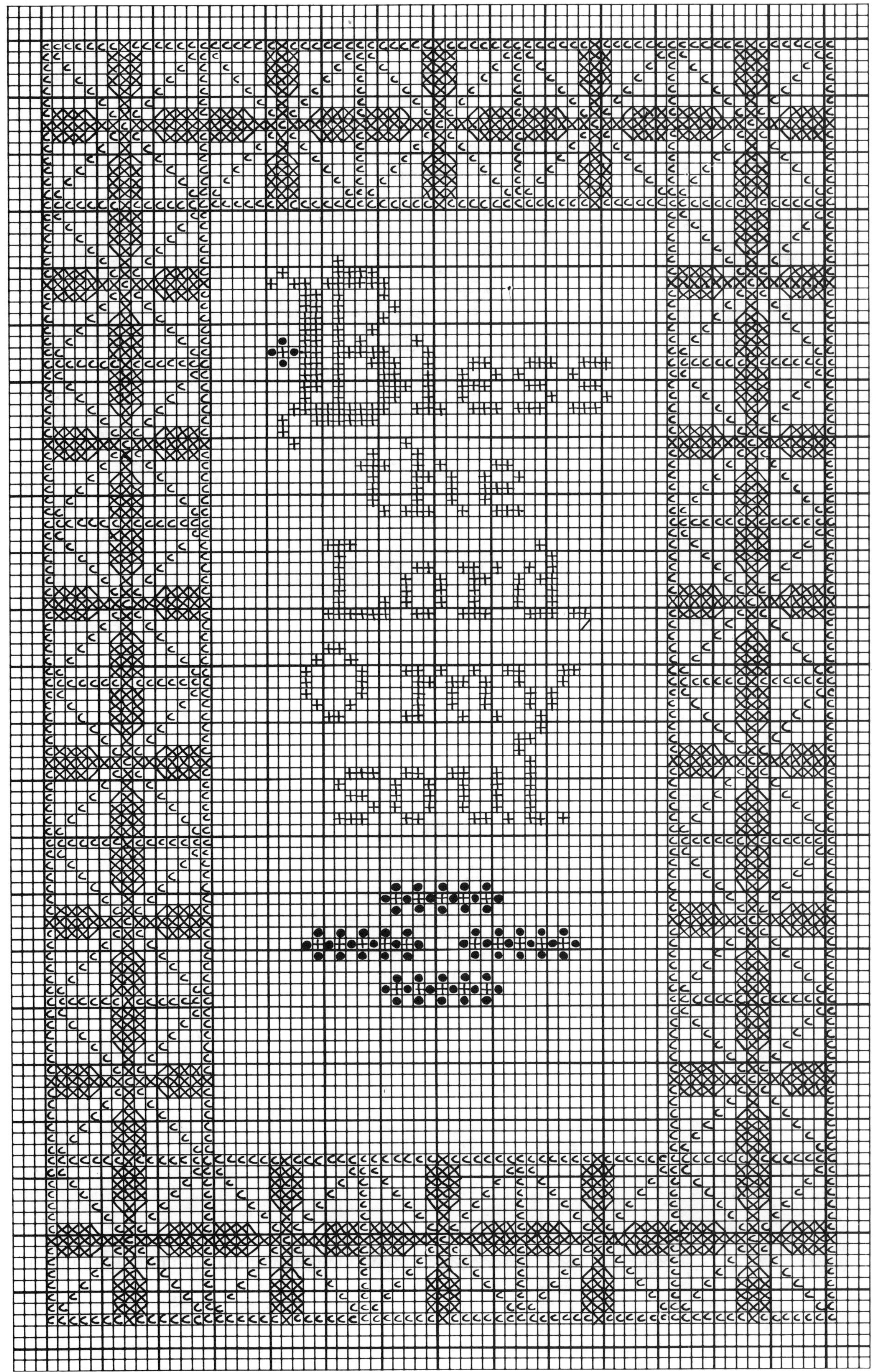

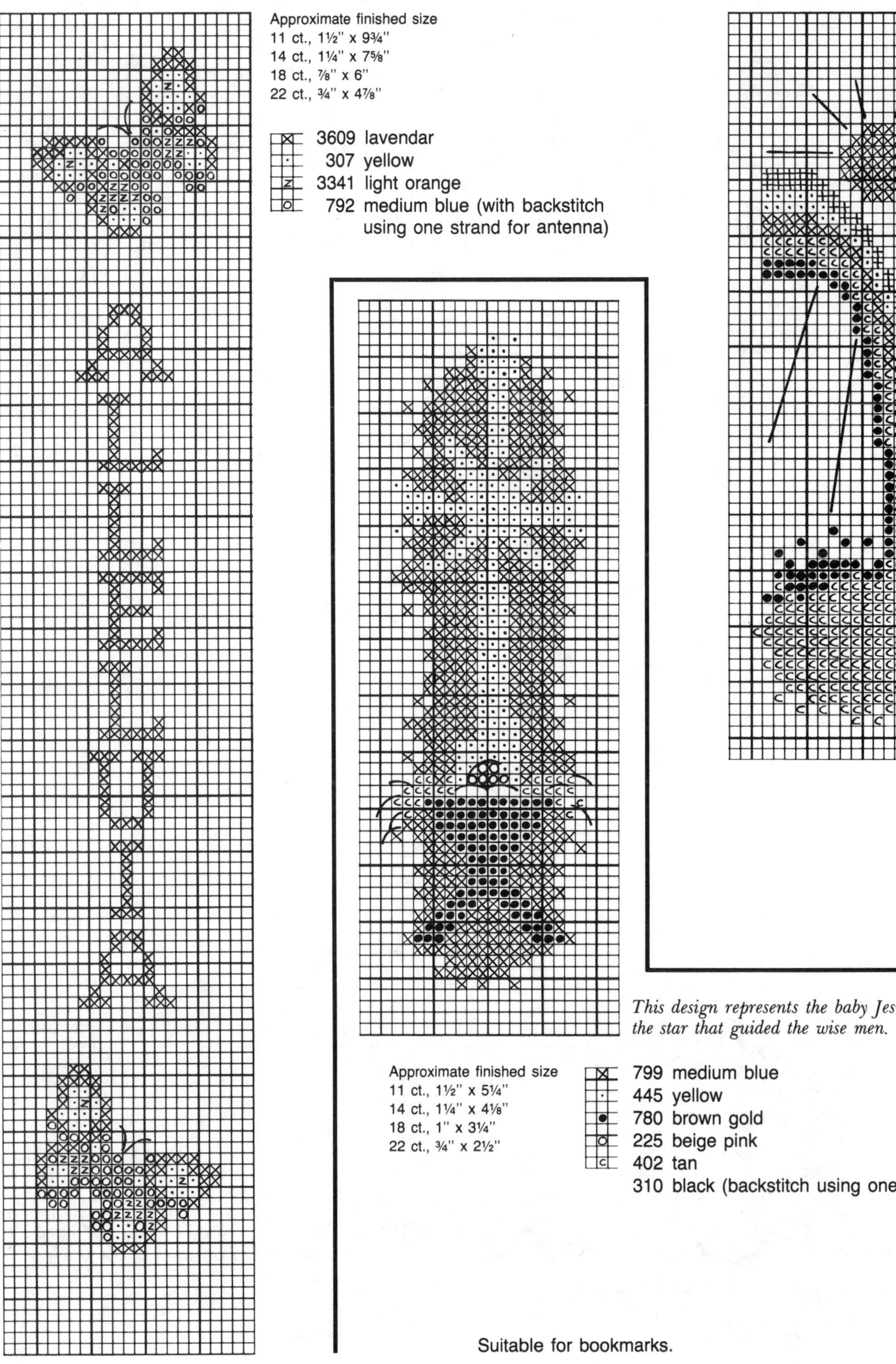

Approximate finished size
11 ct., 1½" x 9¾"
14 ct., 1¼" x 7⅝"
18 ct., ⅞" x 6"
22 ct., ¾" x 4⅞"

Symbol	DMC	Color
X	3609	lavendar
·	307	yellow
Z	3341	light orange
O	792	medium blue (with backstitch using one strand for antenna)

This design represents the baby Jesus and the star that guided the wise men.

Approximate finished size
11 ct., 1½" x 5¼"
14 ct., 1¼" x 4⅛"
18 ct., 1" x 3¼"
22 ct., ¾" x 2½"

Symbol	DMC	Color
X	799	medium blue
·	445	yellow
●	780	brown gold
O	225	beige pink
C	402	tan
	310	black (backstitch using one strand)

Suitable for bookmarks.

The rainbow represents God's promise to Noah. It assures us of God's love.

Approximate finished size
11 ct., 1½" x 5¼"
14 ct., 1¼" x 4⅛"
18 ct., 1" x 3¼"
22 ct., ¾" x 2½"

Symbol	Color
☒	307 medium yellow (with backstitch)
·	740 medium orange
+	900 red orange
●	827 light blue
c	704 light green

Symbol	Color
//	433 brown
■	317 gray (stem stitch using one or two strands for antennae)
·	445 yellow
+	3341 light orange
●	3687 dark rose
c	3689 light pink
☒	992 medium blue green
✳	310 black
o	white (if using colored material)

Approximate finished size
11 ct., 6¾" x 5⅝"
14 ct., 5⅜" x 4⅝"
18 ct., 4⅛" x 3½"
22 ct., 3⅜" x 3"

The butterfly represents Christ's resurrection.

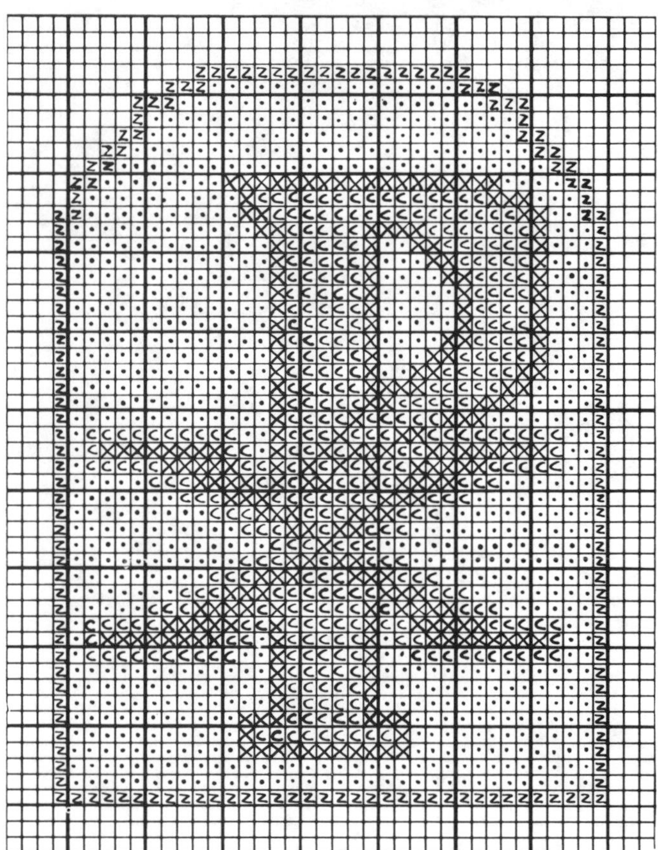

The oldest monogram for Jesus Christ is the Chi-Rho. This monogram is formed by placing the Greek letters X (Chi) and P (Rho) together. These are the first two letters of the Greek word for Christ.

Jesus is all the world to me

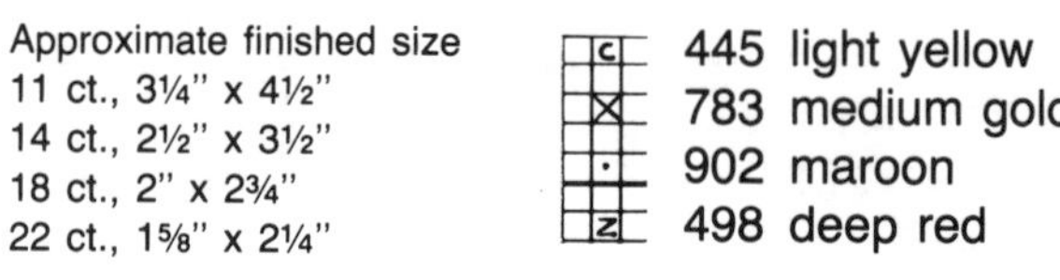

Approximate finished size
11 ct., 3¼" x 4½"
14 ct., 2½" x 3½"
18 ct., 2" x 2¾"
22 ct., 1⅝" x 2¼"

c 445 light yellow
X 783 medium gold
· 902 maroon
z 498 deep red

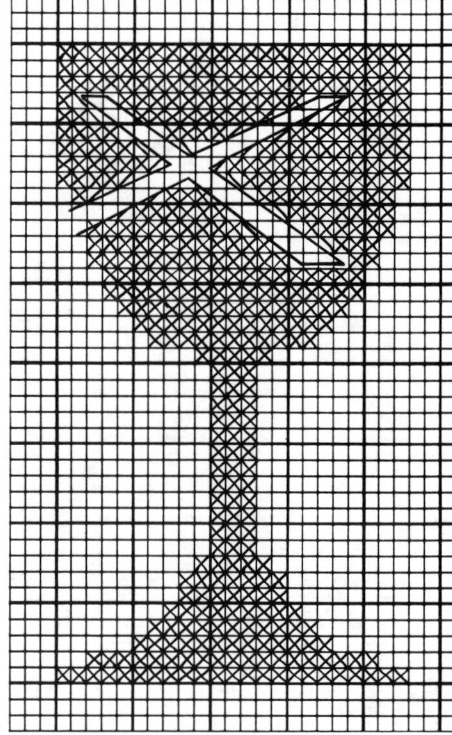

Emblem of the Christian Church (Disciples of Christ)

Approximate finished size
11 ct., 2" x 3½"
14 ct., 1⅝" x 2¾"
18 ct., 1¼" x 2⅛"
22 ct., 1" x 1¾"

X 666 red
black (outline cross using one or two strands)

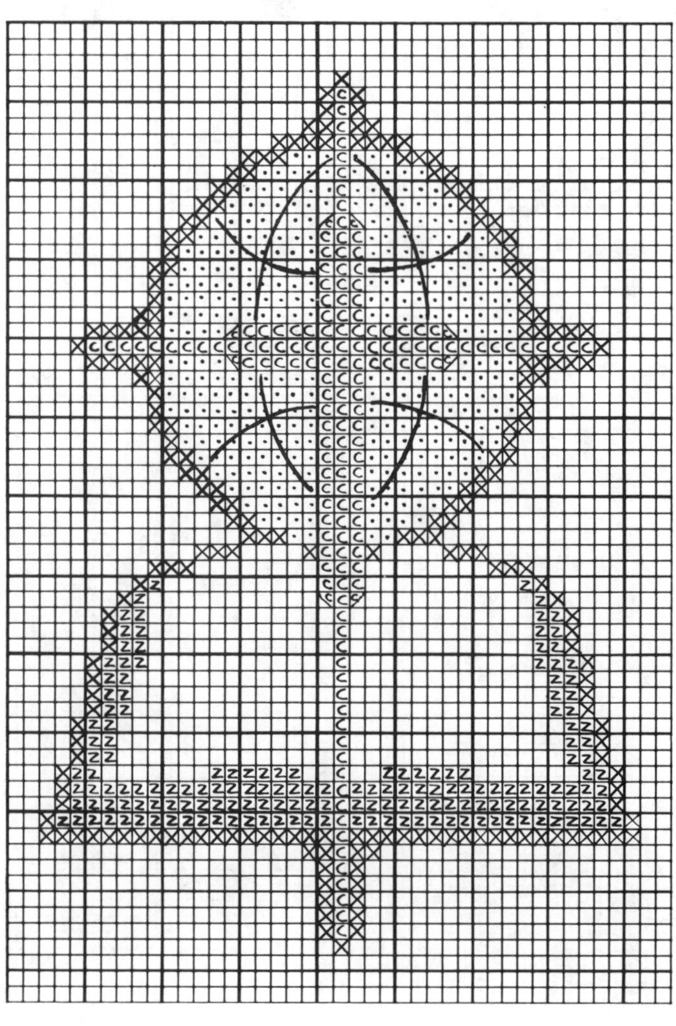

Emblem of the Southern Baptist Convention

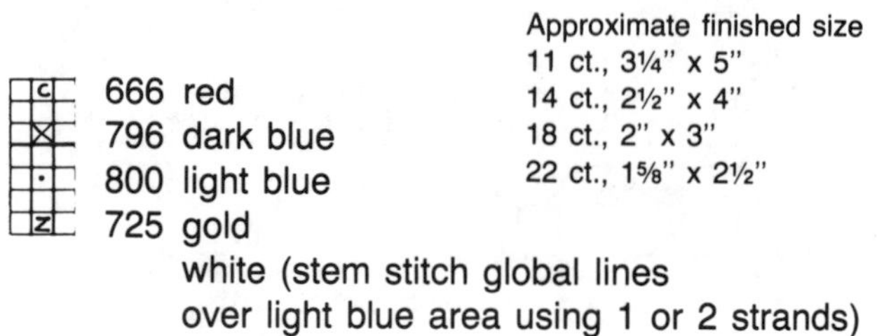

Approximate finished size
11 ct., 3¼" x 5"
14 ct., 2½" x 4"
18 ct., 2" x 3"
22 ct., 1⅝" x 2½"

c 666 red
X 796 dark blue
· 800 light blue
z 725 gold
white (stem stitch global lines over light blue area using 1 or 2 strands)

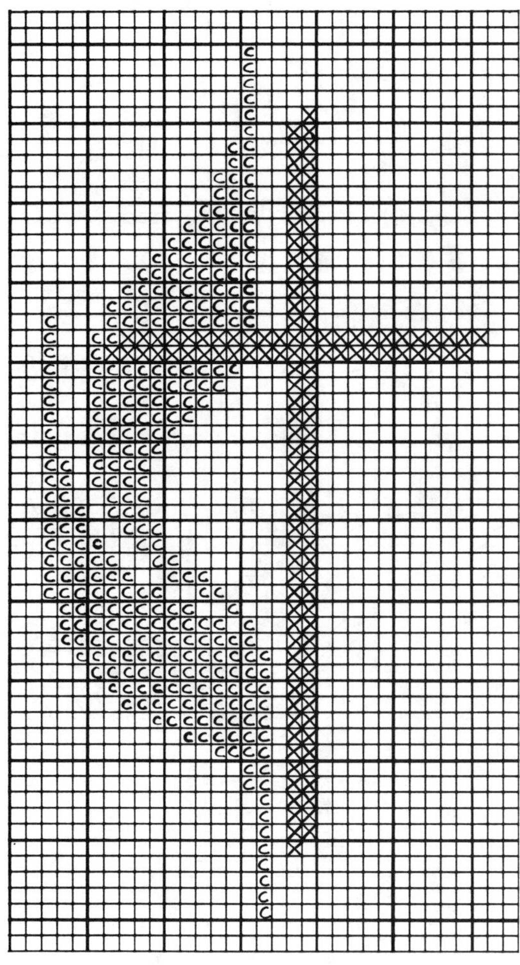

Emblem of The United Methodist Church

Approximate finished size
11 ct., 2⅝" x 5"
14 ct., 2" x 4"
18 ct., 1⅝" x 3"
22 ct., 1⅜" x 2½"

Symbol	Color
c	666 red
X	black

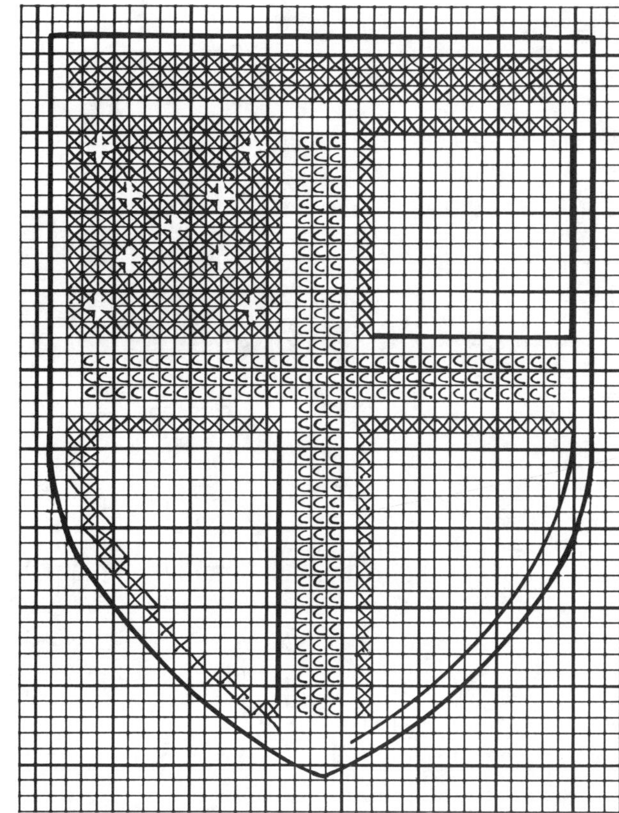

Emblem of the Episcopal Church

Approximate finished size
11 ct., 3¼" x 4⅛"
14 ct., 2½" x 3¼"
18 ct., 2" x 2½"
22 ct., 1⅝" x 2"

Symbol	Color
X	796 dark blue (with stem stitch)
c	666 red
	white (stitch crosses over blue cross-stitched area)

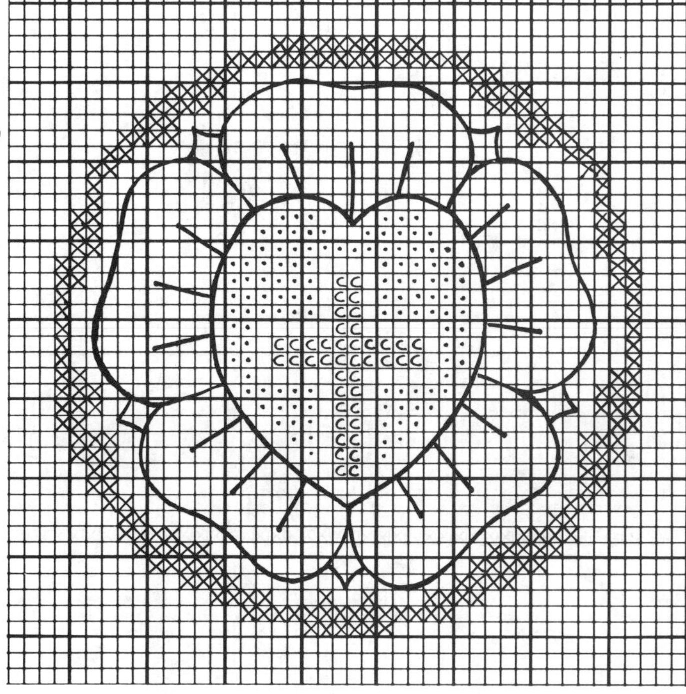

Emblem of the Lutheran Church

Approximate finished size
11 ct., 3½"
14 ct., 2¾"
18 ct., 2⅛"
22 ct., 1¾"

Symbol	Color
X	800 light blue
c	796 dark blue
·	666 red
	725 gold (stem stitch outline of flower using one or two strands)

The peacock is a symbol of the Resurrection. His gorgeous tail feathers will drop off, but even more attractive feathers grow to take their place, symbolizing new life from death.

Christ the Lord is risen today.

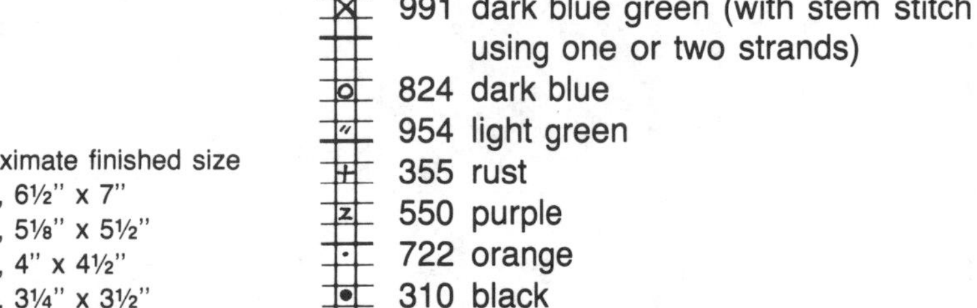

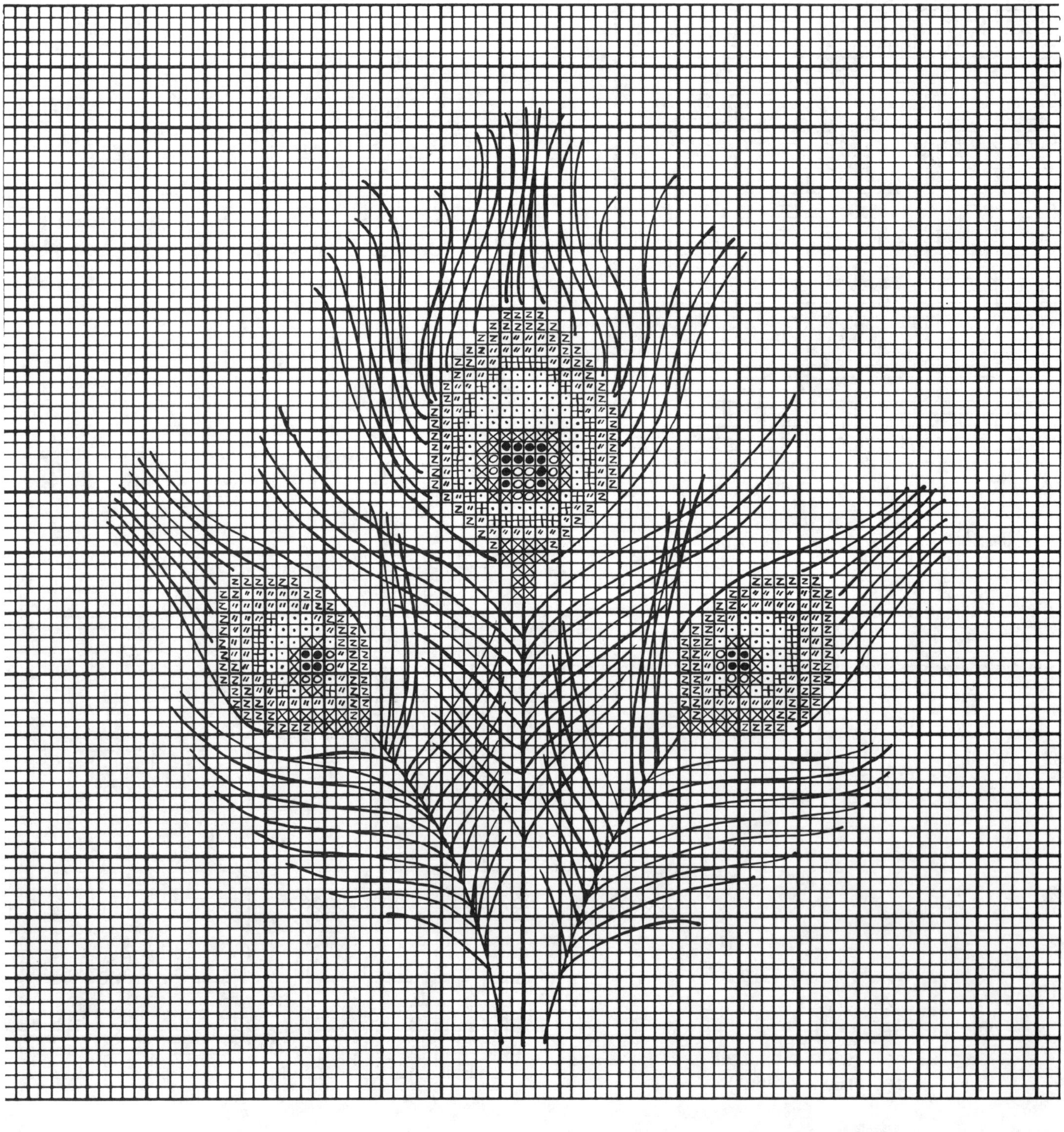

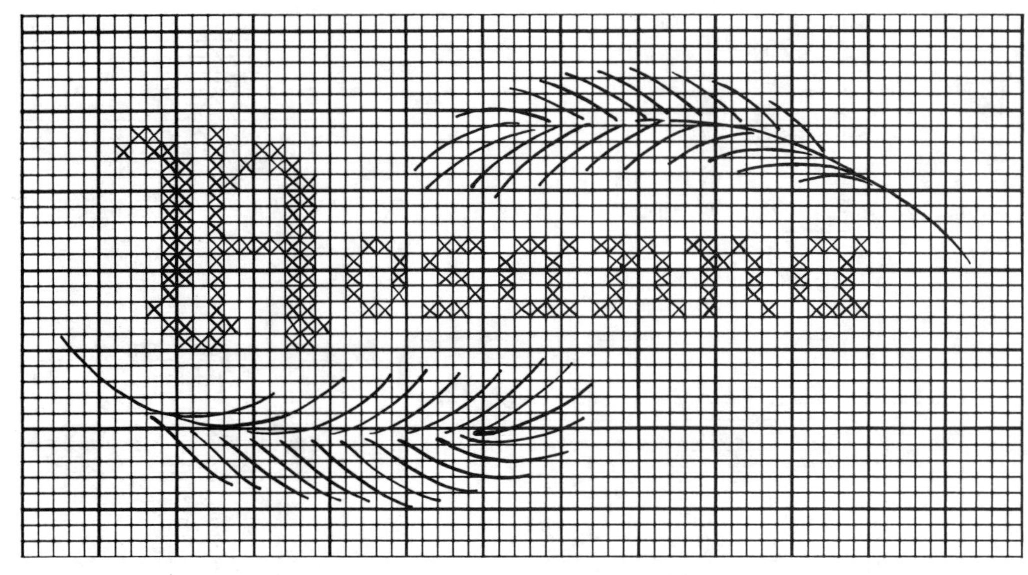

Approximate finished size
11 ct., 5⅝" x 2⅝"
14 ct., 4½" x 2"
18 ct., 3½" x 1⅝"
22 ct., 2¾" x 1¼"

metalic gold
986 green (stem stitch palms)

IHS are the first three letters (iota, eta, sigma) of the Greek spelling of Jesus.

Approximate finished size
11 ct., 6¾" x 5"
14 ct., 5⅜" x 4"
18 ct., 4⅛" x 3"
22 ct., 3⅜" x 2½"

744 yellow
758 medium salmon
3685 maroon
797 bright blue

In its early life the butterfly grows a smooth, hard shell (chrysalis) which appears to be dead. Inside, the butterfly continues to grow and in about two weeks breaks free and flies away. Because of this, the butterfly is a popular resurrection symbol.

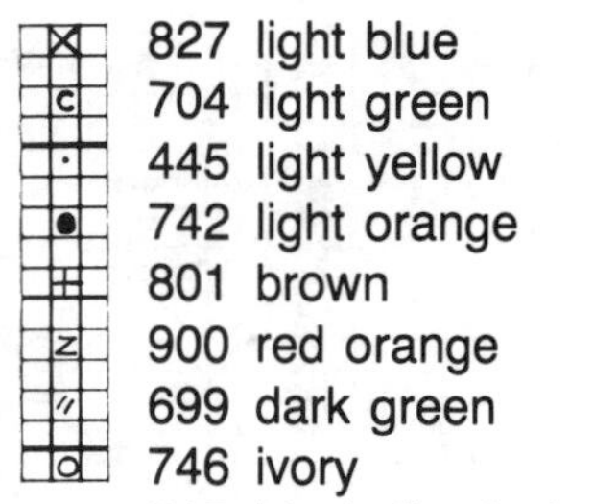

827 light blue
704 light green
445 light yellow
742 light orange
801 brown
900 red orange
699 dark green
746 ivory
310 black (backstitch using one strand)

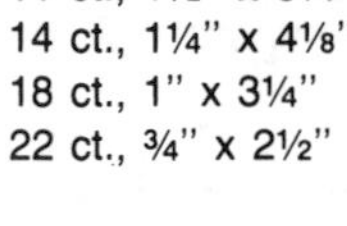

Approximate finished size
11 ct., 1½" x 5¼"
14 ct., 1¼" x 4⅛"
18 ct., 1" x 3¼"
22 ct., ¾" x 2½"

Suitable for bookmark.

This design shows the lamb (Jesus) no longer wounded, but standing with the banner of victory, suggesting the victorious nature of his sacrifice.

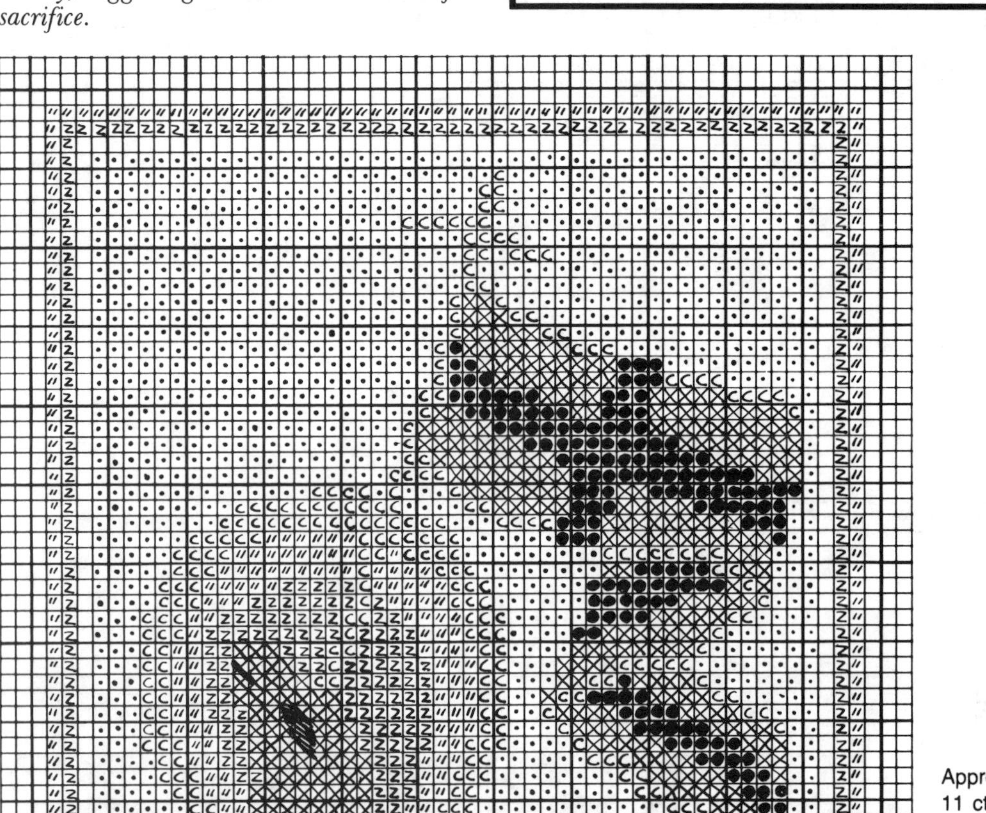

Approximate finished size
11 ct., 4¾" x 8¼"
14 ct., 3¾" x 6½"
18 ct., 2⅞" x 5"
22 ct., 2⅜" x 4⅛"

312 medium dark blue
744 yellow
742 yellow orange
722 orange
304 red
310 black (satin stitch)
white

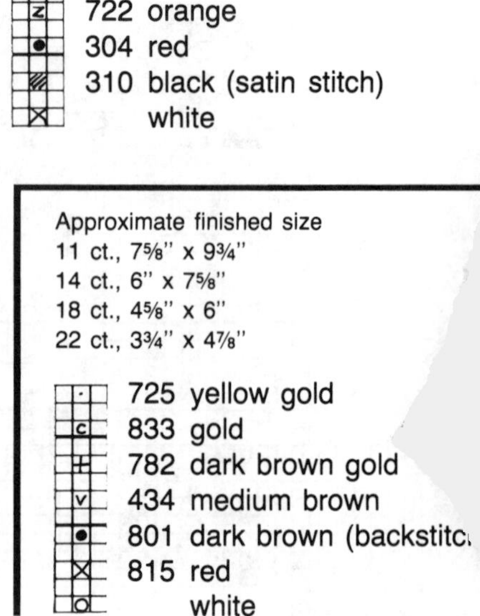

Approximate finished size
11 ct., 7⅝" x 9¾"
14 ct., 6" x 7⅝"
18 ct., 4⅝" x 6"
22 ct., 3¾" x 4⅞"

725 yellow gold
833 gold
782 dark brown gold
434 medium brown
801 dark brown (backstitc
815 red
white

Christ the Lord
Is King

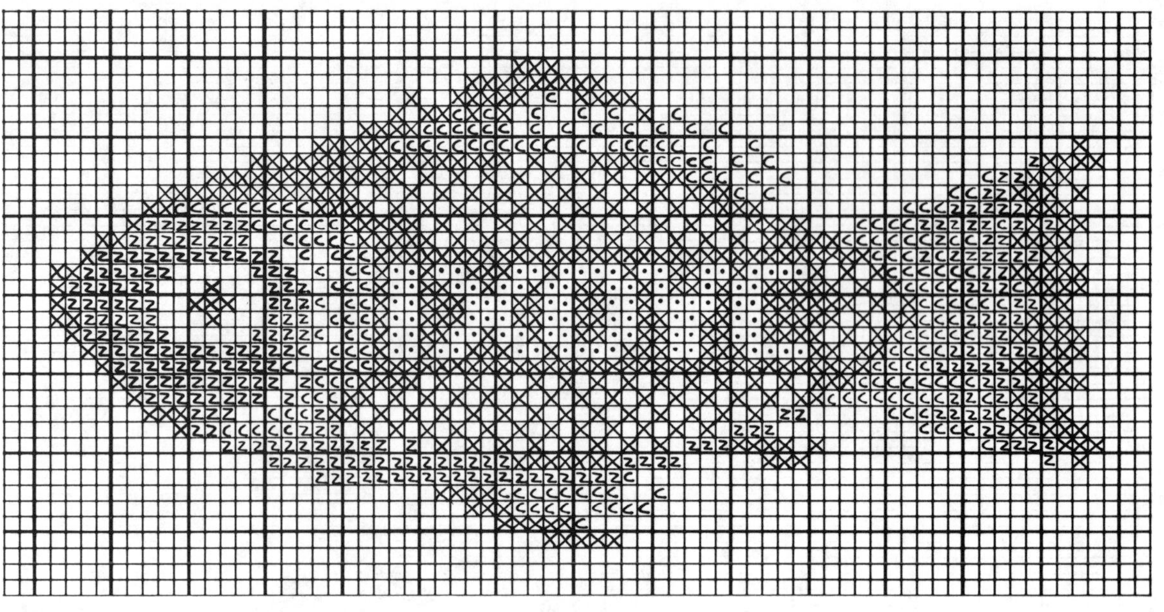

The fish was a secret sign used by early, persecuted Christians to designate themselves as believers in Jesus. The initial letters of the Greek words for "Jesus Christ, God's Son, Saviour" spell the Greek word for fish.

Approximate finished size
11 ct., 6¼" x 3"
14 ct., 4¾" x 2¼"
18 ct., 3¾" x 1¾"
22 ct., 3¼" x 1½"

- · 727 light yellow
- c 827 light blue
- z 954 light green
- X 991 blue green

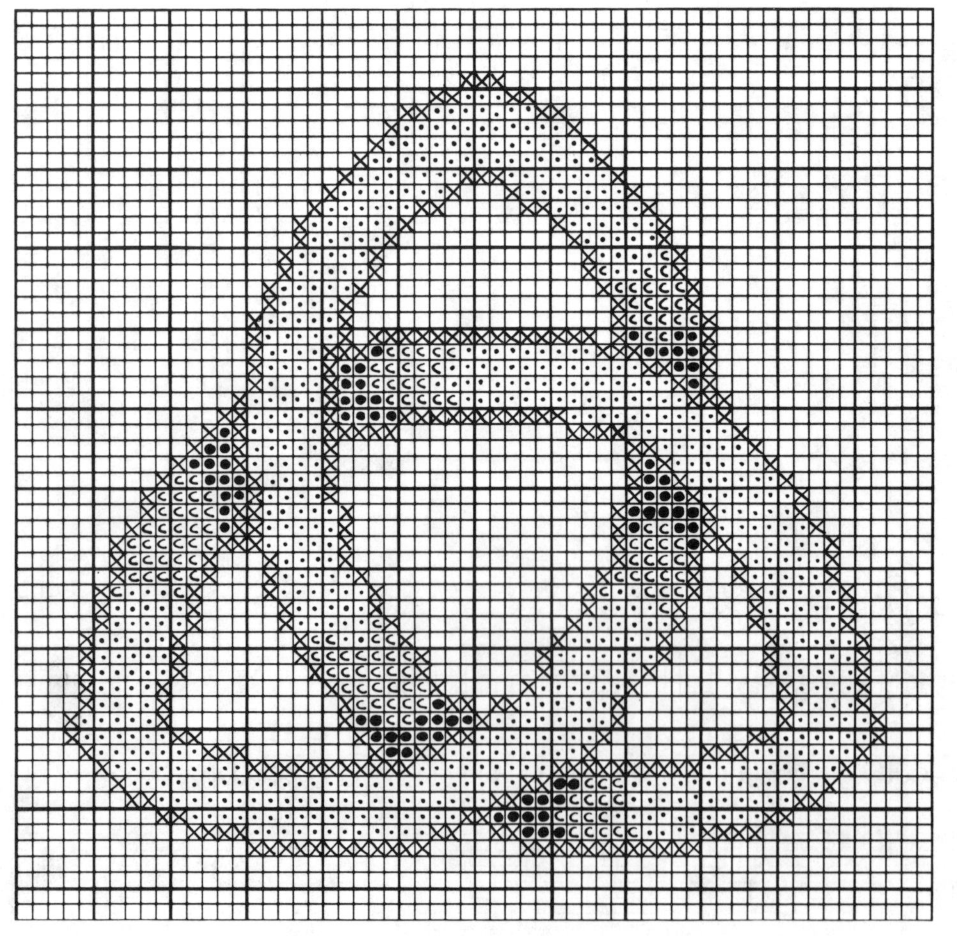

Symbol of the Holy Trinity

Approximate finished size
11 ct., 4⅞" x 4½"
14 ct., 3⅞" x 3½"
18 ct., 3" x 2¾"
22 ct., 2⅜" x 2¼"

- · 445 light yellow
- c 307 bright yellow
- ● 742 light orange
- X white

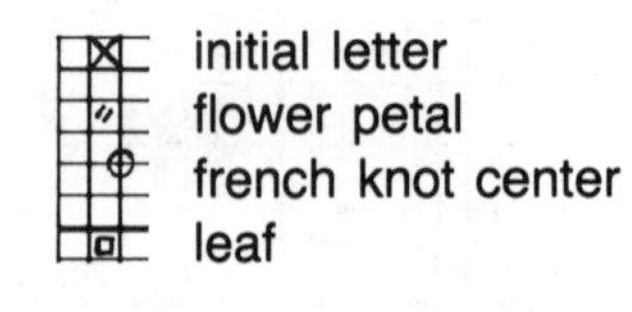

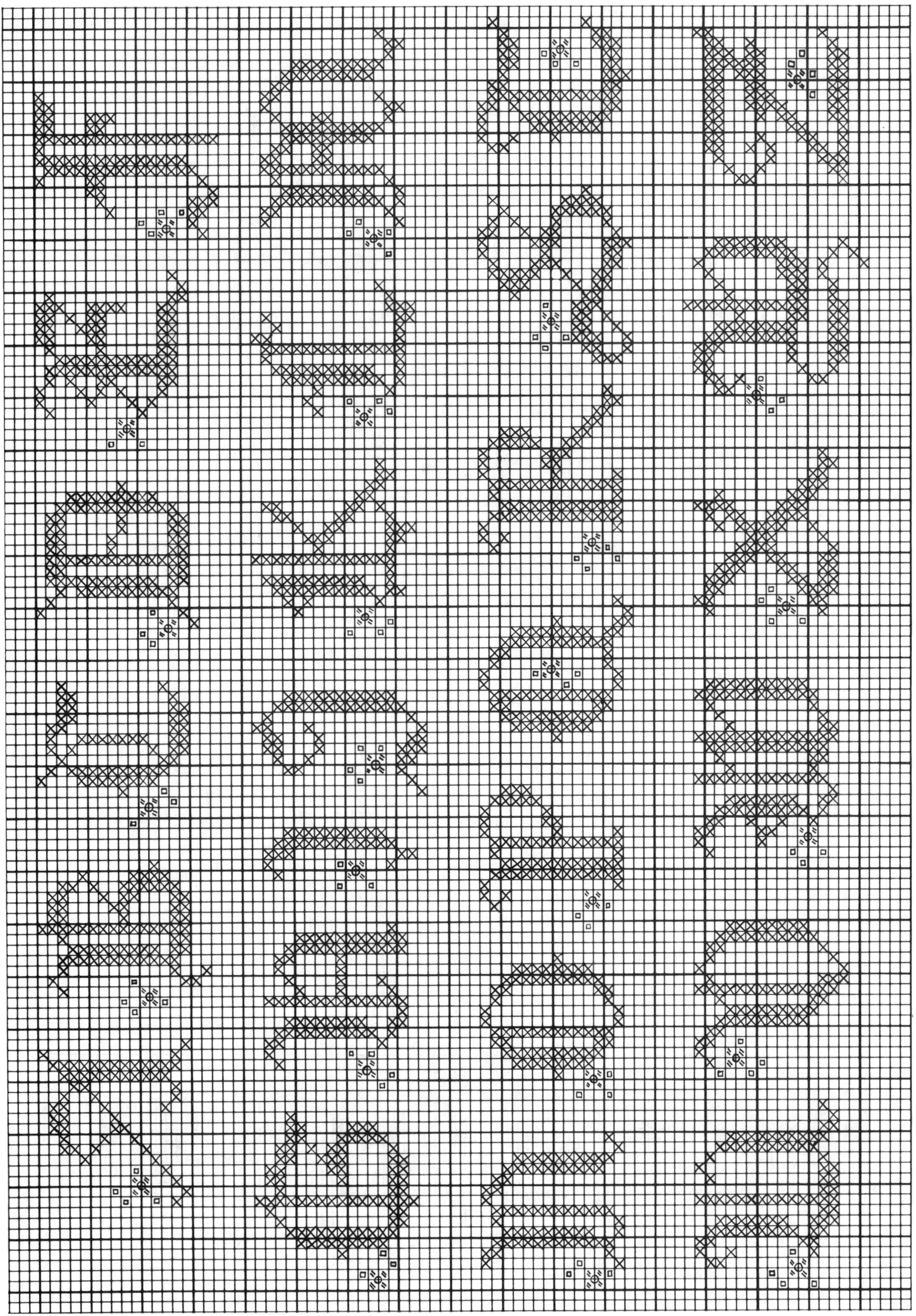

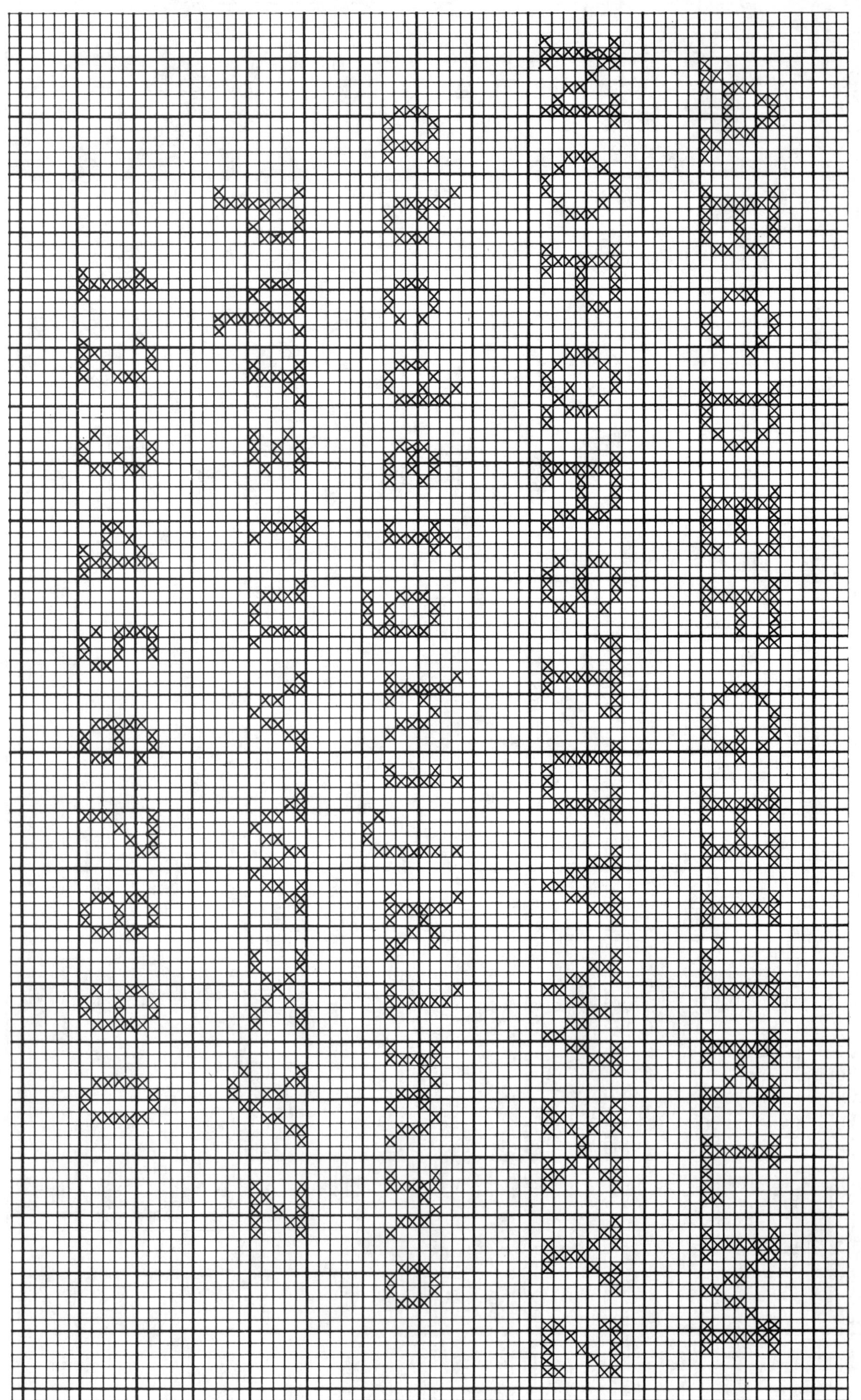